Carcharhinus leucas

Zachary Webb Nicholls

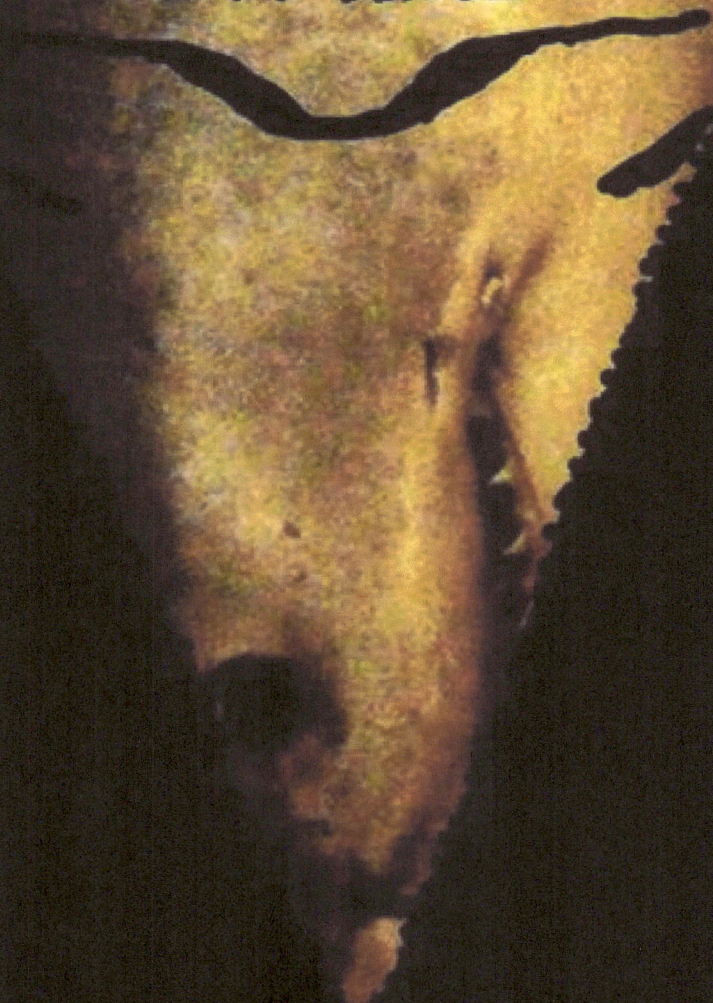

Carcharhinus leucas
Copyright © 2014 by Zachary Webb Nicholls (Dr. Jaws)

All rights reserved. Published in the United States by Deep Sea Publishing LLC, Herndon, Virginia.

ISBN-13: 978-1-939535-63-4
ISBN: 1939535638
E-Book ISBN-13: 978-1-939535-64-1
E-Book ISBN: 1939535646

www.deepseapublishing.com

Printed in the United States of America

Hello friend,

What you are about to read is secret.

Each word, picture, and symbol has a meaning, and together they will help you find something very strange, but very exciting. Furthermore, each word, picture, and symbol is anchored in a living truth, but in order to fully understand what that truth is, you need to do some exploring.

Beyond this little book, there is a boundless, bountiful wealth of knowledge within your reach. You of course are not required to seek it, but if you do, I assure you will be rewarded with a richer understanding of our shark, the seas, and the mystery of life itself.

For now, you hold in your hands a map. Let it take you—from the past, to the present, to the weird—deep into an ocean of legends, of dark wonders, and of amber eyes…

….let it take you to Shark.

Carcharhinus

leucas

Praised be Goliath

King of the River

Lord of Blood

Whose eye is ever watching

And whose maw broke

The reign of Niloticus

The Great Serpent King

Whose rule was unjust

And whose appetite

Was insatiable

Starlight is finite
A star has a time to end
Explosive its death

Scattered star pieces
Combine into the combined
Birth of sun and earth

Sun fire creates
With calm earth, air, and water
Life elemental

~ *Domain Eukarya* ~

Imagine a mountain

Cool and calming

Trickling water down its slope

It is serene in its grey

Paint it with a domain

Of life so rich in color

That the eyes will forever wonder

At its design and sustain

A curiosity

Unique only to Eukarya

When cell within cell became cell itself

So long ago, a peak

In life was reached

From origins so humble

Came oranges so fiery

With jades, emeralds, and harlequins each

Beauties of the forest

Protecting the ambling reds

And boisterous blues

With calming arms best

Suited for shading

Amber-centered violets

And cinnabar-sighted mosaics

All art never fading

This domain is of color

See Eukarya

Splendid and diverse

Muses of the world

For the art that it is

~Kingdom Animalia~

Look what the dawn has broken

Something new stirs in the seas

A novel language now spoken

The animals have come to be

~

From one tiny sponge to one funny man

A simple life will always be banned

A drama that we cannot understand

The animals, come and play, come and play

A hardworking ant meets an unfriendly beetle

While two birds romance, it seems nothing's
sweeter

A seahorse's dance is such a unique love

Animals, come and play, come and play

~

Embrace the feeling of life

A body that's one from many

A hunger that sets you right

~

And chase in manner uncanny

Your strange sweet compassions

You animal, go and play, go and play

~Phylum Chordata~

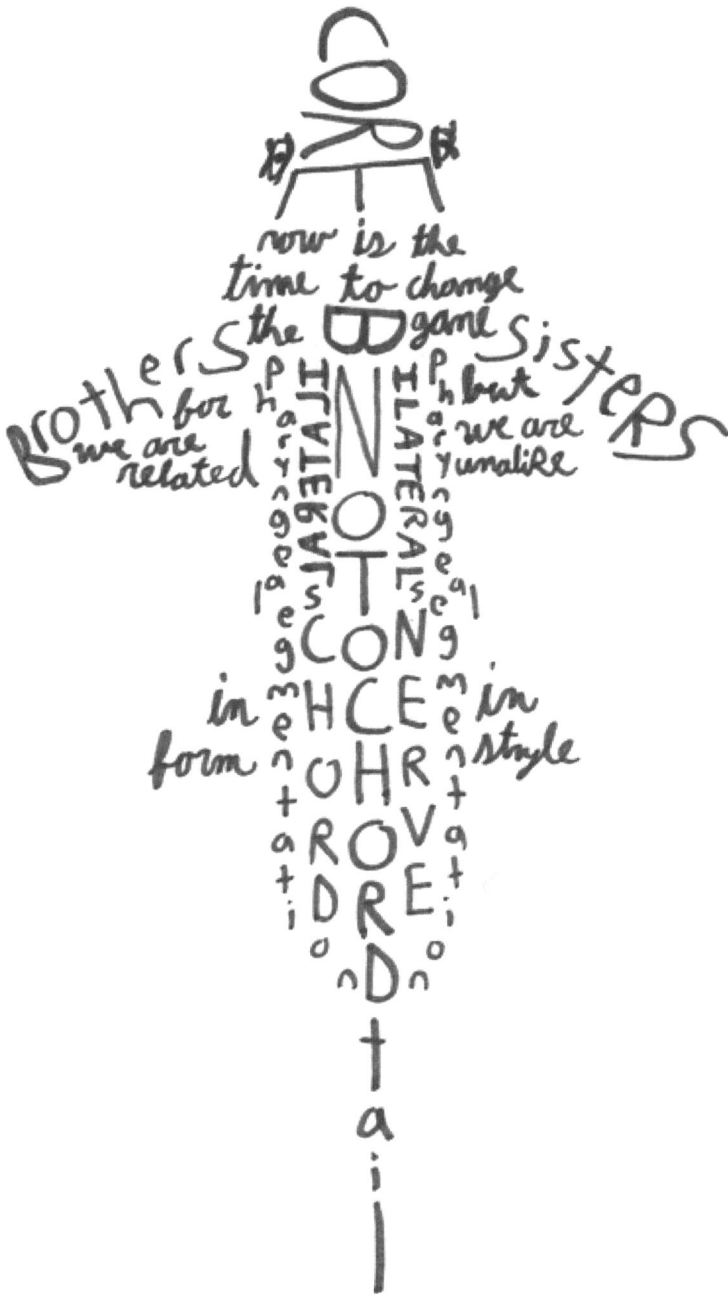

CORD

now is the
time to change
the game

Brothers   Sisters

for   but
we are   we are
related   unalike

pharyngeal slits   bilateral symmetry

NOTOCHORD

CONCE...
in   HCE   in
form   OHR   style
            ROVE
            DRE;
            ...D...

tail

~ *Class Chondrichthyes* ~

There is a hall of marble and limestone—of honor and ocean—adorned with obsidian shadows; the Chondrichthyan Silhouettes. Each Silhouette is an embodiment of form and essence, said to be constructed by the gods to remind the world of the Living Shadows; the chimaera, the ray, and the shark.

Believed to be guardians of both the ocean and the human soul, The Living Shadows served to consume the weaknesses of each. Through so doing, they culled corruption and protected the life of both soul and sea.

To honor this nobility cloaked in ferocity, the Chondrichthyan Silhouettes are each adorned with an eye of pearl and gemstone. Together, body and eye capture the essence of a Living Shadow:

A power cooled with grace

An immortal who could die

A legend with a heartbeat.

~Order Carcharhiniformes~

Beauteous beasts of time

A standard and yet an ideal

Coasting beyond the sands

And into depths of teal

For fear they do not

As in their eyes reveal

An ancient secret light

Seen only by those who feel

Akin to their plight

And akin to their strength

A cutting edge of blue

A coursing blood of length

By such eyes as theirs
Which close upon a kill
They form their sacred forms
The fears that we've instilled

These rare and common types
Of shark will always be
As changing as the tides
But still masters of the sea

~Family Carcharhinidae~

The requiem sharks
Aqua volcanoes aware
Powerful but calm

~*Genus Carcharhinus*~

SHARPNOSE

"Scrqr d lkjqderp sk ur scr qsmjempe qcmpgq; scry mpr ikqs djsrpswdjre wdsc ctimjdsy, mje mpr scr qstaa ka hrbrjeq."

Note: The above is a keyword cypher. The keyword is hidden on the following page. Use it to unlock a smaller insight.

19

The White One

Müller & Henle, 1839

Carcharhinus leucas

A medium-sized shark with an average mass of 110kg. It is distinguished by its heavy body, small eyes, and lack of an interdorsal ridge. The dorsal and pectoral fins are semifalcate.

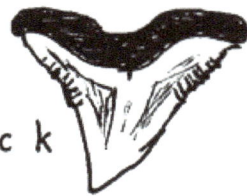

Bull Shark   Tiburón sarda

قرش الثور   公牛鯊   オオメジロザメ

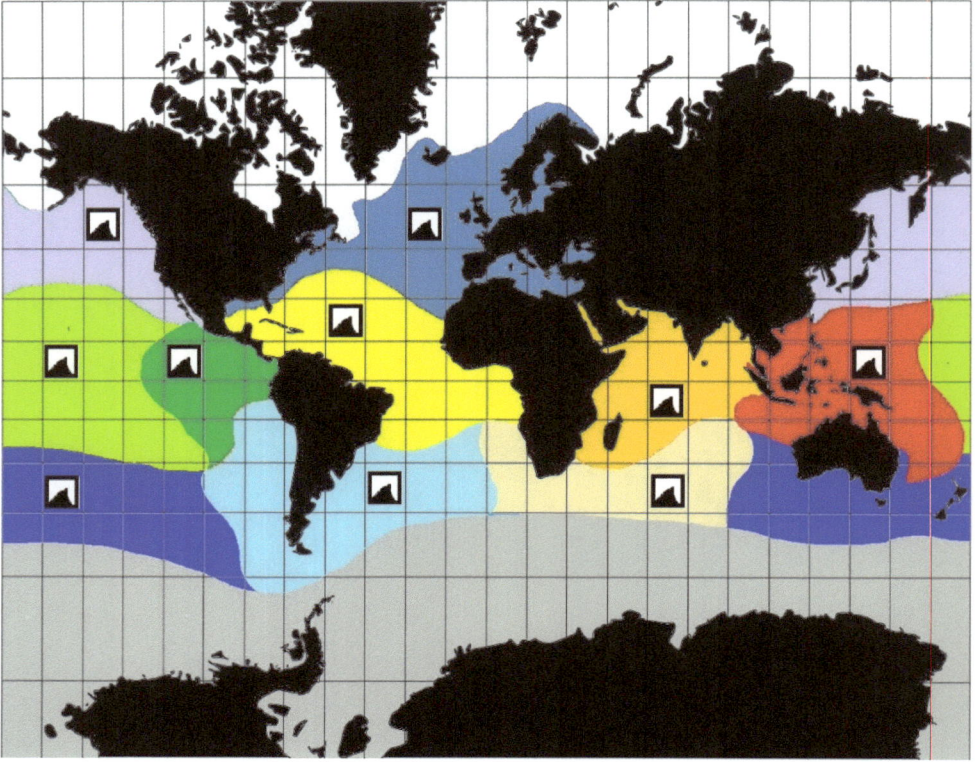

~*Global Distribution*~

North Akula Sea

Tempest Requin Sea

Wild Zame Sea

Sunset Sea of Reken

Colorful Sea of Sarka

Bountiful Sea of Shayu

Peaceful Sea of Mano

Sunrise Sea of Tiburon

Grande Tubarao Sea

Groot Haai Sea

Great Shark Sea

South Sarko Sea

~Haunts~

Carcharhinus leucas

can be found in the following zones:

Littoral   Neritic
Sunlit

And the following special habitats:

Freshwater

~

"Legends are made in truth as well as lies. Both lie and truth give legend life, though life itself is legend without lie. The dispatch of life, the dethronement of the king...each was lie made real by the devouring of the impossibility: the sudden grip and seizure of mortality universal. The lie of immortality was made truth by the king, and this untruth brought the possibility of his death which, when realized, showed all how legend was truly born."

~ *Habits* ~

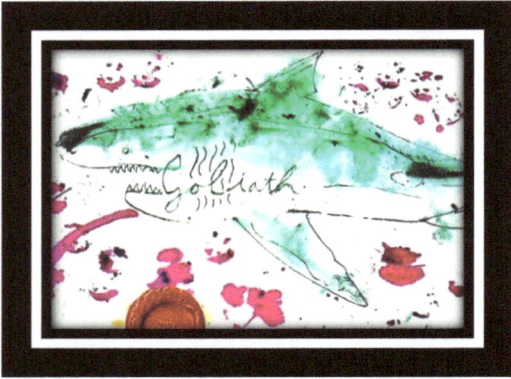

Carcharhinus leucas is most famous for its rare ability to tolerate freshwater and travel thousands of kilometers upriver in the great tributaries of the world. The shark may appear sluggish as it patrols the seabed, but when enticed by prey, it becomes dangerously agile and quick.

Carcharhinus leucas has an extremely broad appetite, and is known to consume other sharks. It is one of the 'Fatal Four' as it has attacked and killed humans with its power and precarious proximity.

~ *Humanity* ~

Carcharhinus leucas is to be perceived as a

DANGEROUS SHARK

In light of the concerning attributes that follow;

Its threatening proximity to man

Its fearsome size and dentition

Its relatively plentiful abundance

These attributes are presented with the truth that
Carcharhinus leucas has been implicated in

DOZENS of FATAL ATTACKS

As a resource, the shark is a popular aquarium subject
and a significant ecotourism attraction.

~

However, man has fished Carcharhinus leucas and
polluted many of the rivers in which it calls home.

As a result, Carcharhinus leucas is a

SUSCEPTIBLE SPECIES

~ *Goliath* ~

"A tale about our shark, and yet much more...."

Before the Age of Goliath the great river was in tyranny.

Before the Age of Goliath, Niloticus -- son of Vulgaris, son of Dylus -- was King of the River of Good Omens…king of us the meek and remorseful of his reign. Niloticus was fate universal; he chose the time of his subject's passing into the nether, and he chose unfairly.

Those who feared this Great Serpent King were wise.

Those who revolted were devoured.

So was the life of the river…before our vindication by another.…

In the seventh month of the seventh year of the Niloctus reign, a stranger exotic and untamed entered our world. Against the river's course, he broke into our time with massive power, inexplicable might, but as a shadow…a ghost so large it could not be measured. Just as the darkness of the twilight sun spreads, piercing with time into the far corners of the river, so too did the presence of this stranger penetrate into our minds, and we shuddered at his novel call; Goliath, the Bringer of Shadows, the Consumer of the Corrupt, entered our world and sought the monster he would come to dispatch.

No being warned him of the powers of Niloticus.

No soul dared to approach Goliath, for he too was powerful.

Well matched were the opponents. Though each meant to draw from the other the blood of regality, the inherent ability to dominate, each still faced the obstacle of the other's will and power.

Power matched well with power.

Niloticus the Horrendous was gigantic, and plated with armor thicker than stone. Indeed, his very coat was of rocks and boulders, mountains and crevasses, slopes so perfect and unbreakable that he surely was born from the Earth itself. His tail was itself a monstrosity, worming its owner silently through the murk so as to deceive the many and slay the many. It was of spikes refined—an evil creation—and it served him well against the river's will.

Doubtless the most dangerous distinction of Niloticus the Unending was his maw. That great, hulking wonder of death, half the size of the entire behemoth, rimmed with flawlessly smooth, ivory stalactites and stalagmites, oh so willing to puncture even the softest of flesh. The maw that ended the bison, the hippos, the lion's cub and the lioness herself…the maw that destroyed us and our brothers, our chances for life beyond life, for progeny, for legacy…that maw was an evil unto itself, sprung loose and wild upon the world, unrestrained and un-orchestrated, a freak of a thing broken from its creator's grasp.

Goliath may not have known the task which he faced and the power of the beast to stop him, but he too was blessed with attributes both horrendous and sublime.

Undetectable were the flawless chain-links of his skin, curved and cutting so as to grant the leviathan unmatchable speed. His tail and fins were built to cleave the ocean's crashing waves— to bisect the grey so as to most quickly arrive at the red. His eyes were persistent and bright, small suns alive with the fire of dispatch. But most incredible of all, behind the hulking mass of his jaw, were Goliath's unending teeth.

Each was sharp enough to face its task: to strip away the armor of The Serpent King and thereby defeat him. Each was perfectly cut, a pearl too deadly to touch, rimmed with smaller indentations to aid in the shearing. Though they hid comfortably within Goliath's mouth, they were in a second's notice ready for a killing strike, and they numbered a thousand.

But unbeknownst to all of us at the time, Goliath possessed a final talent that no mortal could sensibly comprehend; the ability to see the unseen. Without sight, sense, or touch, Goliath the Miraculous could find the heart of his enemy, and count exactly the number of its beat. Truly he was a remnant of the supernatural, a final defender of the world's mythology…Goliath the Soulseeker, The Undefeated and Impossible, Master of the Forbidden Powers, was destined with his wonders to slay the evil king of our world.

Met they at the Point of Reeds: the northern gate of the Niloticus the Maleficent's kingdom. Slumbering was he, the tyrant of our realm, but with open eyes that never betrayed its owner's will. None attempted to read the eyes of Niloticus; they were black without life, but hid the cunning of their very much living master.

Goliath, however, could instantly tempt the eyes to tell him their secrets, and upon his advent persuaded them to reveal the state of the sleeping beast ashore. The Great Serpent indeed had been slumbering, but was soon to wake from troubled dreams. Undetectable to us, his attitude changed while his body remained still as stone. But Goliath sensed agitation, and adjusted course; he passed the despot with defiance, and boldly circled before him, flashing in the sun the cutting blade that was his back.

Niloticus, at first angered, became amused at the thought of facing a worthy challenge to his throne, and watched with sickening pleasure as the newcomer presented his might.

The arrogance of the beast polluted the water.

Goliath then knew full well that The Tyrant Lizard King intended to meet him, and he thus prepared for contest. Arched was his heavy back, breaking the muddy brackishness that concealed his truly monstrous size; sharply he turned to pass again through the watch of his enemy, and upon this second transgression Niloticus entered the water.

Crimson did the sky turn. Calm did the waters become as they anticipated the coming duel. We ourselves huddled together and watched from safe distance as the challenge of our age was about to unfold.

Niloticus came into his enemy's presence and formed with him the circle of the duel. As slowly as the stars emerged they circled, each patiently waiting for the mistake of the other. Niloticus was well aged and exuded the confidence of experience, the very few scars of the very many past battles. Goliath was younger, but knew of life outside the river kingdom: the Great Beyond. From its blue and unending waters did the challenger emerge, and none knew what perils such a place already presented to our massive hero.

Night soon blanketed the land, and the crescent moon demanded that a strike be made. Goliath sensed his opponent's impatience, and would take it as advantage.

Niloticus, who unsuccessfuly attempted to wait out his enemy's resolve and thereby find a weakness, replaced his prior amusement with anger again.

The time was now.

The beast that ruled—the monster that chained us to the bottom with fear—lunged with full malice against the leviathan who wished to bring justice to our world. But Goliath knew; with blessings unending he saw that which could not have been predicted, and acted swiftly. As Niloticus moved to crush the spine of his adversary with maw positioned in fully-terrifying wonder, Goliath turned with unbelievable precision onto the back of his aggressor's neck, his thousand-count fangs fully bared, and delivered the bite.

Again each faced the other, resuming the circle, but at this time with a cloud of unholy blood between them.

We gasped in wonder at the impossibility of what had occurred: Goliath indeed would deliver us.

Niloticus was himself amazed at that which before now was inconceivable; he was bit, and blood was surely drawn. Perhaps fear entered his heart for the first time in his sovereignty, but if so, it was brief.

Angry he was.

The behemoth Niloticus shattered the circle and all sense of patience, and lunged again with a mighty roar that grounded us all and surely cracked our bones. Goliath again predicted this fury, and forcefully pushed past his enemy; he slammed The Dragon against the rocks and boulders of the riverbed, and bit where he could.

In this manner did the duel proceed; on and on would Niloticus the Terrible attempt to seize his enemy, but over and over Goliath would manipulate his position, and bite the pebbled mass that was the body of the sovereign until blood seeped from the royal armor.

Finally, after hours of striking..

and anger…

and fatigue…

…the once-great king slipped away.

As the red river drifted down towards the sea, so too did the power of our oppressor, and we became free. The body was now at the disposal of the aggressor, and so as to solidify his dominance, and prove to our disbelieving eyes that our evil monarch had indeed perished, Goliath the Absolute consumed the remains, and Niloticus, the Great Vile King and unjust judge of our time, was no more.

Now was the Age of Goliath.

Or so we are told. For this very day, no trace of either he or his mighty enemy remains. The river ebbs and flows with peace, and the occasional crocodile or sea fish indeed enters at will, but to no real power as that which was described here in the Account of Goliath.

'What happened to him?' ask I. 'How could he have disappeared when he accomplished such miraculous wonders?' None of the elders truly knew, but some recounted the visions of their ancestors…

"Goliath did rule, and ruled kindly", said one. "He came at whim and left when he decided. He would take what little offering of flesh he needed and nothing more…nothing like the ravenous hunger of the Overlord whom he dispatched. He was a good king, and will return for as long as his current absence."

"No", said another, "Goliath will not return; he did not mean to come into this river at all, and did not intend to face that horrendous monster. Indeed he did save us, but only out of circumstance, not empathy. His challenger came to kill him, and he acted swiftly to deliver us all. He will always be a hero, of course, but I assure you, he will not return."

The Account has been supported.

The Account has been challenged.

Goliath regardless remains elusive to our detection, and maybe never existed at all…nor too Niloticus, perhaps an invention as well…

…though there is one who claims differently.

Asked I the same question, and this one recounted a different tale brought forth from the eyes of his grandfather—eyes that were present at that day of battle.

"He followed Goliath", began this raconteur, "after he witnessed that colossus devour The Great Serpent in the crescent moonlight. Goliath, then in need of slumber himself, left under the cloak of the night, and my grandfather followed him downriver into places he had never before seen or dreamed of.

Past shifting sands and beds of strange greens, above odd creatures both colorful and alarming in their novelty, they drifted together with the aid of the mountain's push and the tide's recess. Of course, my grandfather kept fair distance away from this new king in fear of his unending powers, but Goliath knew of his presence, and it was allowed.

As the sun rose with the dawn of the new era, they approached the mouth of the river: a tumultuous murk demanding the courage of any who trespass into its darkness and depth. My grandfather persisted, but knew that he soon needed to abandon his pursuit of this newfound hero…

Goliath could travel into waters that he simply could not.

Eventually, his audacity was rewarded, and both my grandfather and Goliath the Phenomenal broke free of the river-mouth's murk, and emerged into the clarity and light of the ending blue: the Great Beyond.

It was here that he turned back."

The tone of the bard changed here in unease, and demanded of me to inquire, "Why? Why did he turn back?"

"Because he saw something that confounded him…a terrible, terrifying truth that transformed his understanding of Goliath the Vanquisher, the Undisputed King of the River, the Hero of Our Time".

"And what was this truth?" asked I.

"There is more than one Goliath…" he said, with a truly perturbed heart.

"…in fact, there are thousands."

Respect the seas and all who call them home.

~ *Thanks* ~

"To Tom Davenport, the master of storytelling and all that is Grimm. You have been an unmatchable mentor these past 9 years, and I am honored to have worked with you and to have looked up to you as a guide.

To Andy Murch, who possesses a plethora of powerful photos at Elasmodiver.com; thank you for your stunning shot of Carcharhinus leucas (page 21). It made all the difference.

To those who may be inspired, never trade your inspiration. You can be whomever you want; that choice is always yours. Keep seeking your higher being, and never let go of your love."

~Zachary W. Nicholls
the First Dr. Jaws

www.ingramcontent.com/pod-product-compliance
Lightning Source LLC
Chambersburg PA
CBHW041222270326
41933CB00001B/8